Fathers' Wisdom

THOUGHTS ON LIFE AND FATHERHOOD

Fathers' Wisdom

THOUGHTS ON LIFE AND FATHERHOOD

TRIUMPH
BOOKS
CHICAGO

Library of Congress Cataloging-in-Publication Data

Fathers' wisdom: thoughts on life and fatherhood
        p. cm.
    Includes bibliographical references and index.
    ISBN: 1-57243-381-7
    1. Fathers--Quotations, maxims, etc. 2. Fatherhood--
Quotations, maxims, etc.

PN6084.F3 F39 2000
306.874'2--dc21   00-026675

This book is available in quantity at special discounts for your group or organization. For more information, contact:
Triumph Books
601 South LaSalle Street, Suite 500
Chicago, Illinois 60605
(312) 939-3330
Fax (312) 663-3557

Book design by Roslyn Broder.
Jacket design by Eileen Wagner.

Printed in the United States of America.

TABLE OF CONTENTS

KNIGHTS IN SHINING ARMOR
Fathers

My father was a kingdom seeker. He
believed that the mere act of seeking a
kingdom brought all things unto you . . .

—Adam Clayton Powell Jr.

I learned from the example of my father
that the manner in which one endures what
must be endured is more important than
the thing that must be endured.

—Dean Acheson

[M]y father] taught me that the most powerful
weapon you have is your mind.

—*Andrew Young*

P]apa believed the greatest sin of which we were
capable was to go to bed at night as ignorant as
we had been when we wakened that day.

—*Leo Buscaglia*

I actively opposed ways of life my country
was establishing, and my father before me,
and his father before him.

—*Charles A. Lindbergh Jr.*

My prescription for success is based on
something my father always used to tell me:
you should never try to be better than someone
else, but you should never cease trying to be
the best that you can be.

—*John Wooden*

He stressed to us that it was less important
to be successful and prosperous than it was to
be people of principles, and that you don't
get happy out of accumulating things.
You get happy out of service.

—*Robert F. Kennedy Jr.*

I watched a small man with thick calluses on both hands work fifteen and sixteen hours a day . . . [he] taught me all I needed to know by the simple eloquence of his example.

—*Mario Cuomo*

He instilled in us that what was his was ours, but ultimately what was yours was yours. You've got to work . . .

—*Ed Eckstine, son of jazz great Billy Eckstine*

His heritage to his children wasn't words or
possessions, but an unspoken treasure, the
treasure of his example as a man and a father.
More than anything I have, I'm trying to
pass that on to my children.

—Will Rogers Jr.

My success meant to [my father] everything
he had worked for and believed in was true;
that in America, with hard work and
determination a man can achieve anything.

—Richard Nixon

I was given incentive by my dad, who always
says, 'If you're going to do it, get it done.'

—Charley Pride

My father taught me to work;
he did not teach me to love it.

—*Abraham Lincoln*

Papa . . . used his fists on sharks and fakers,
and all to give his family nice things.

—*Woody Guthrie*

He'd let me walk behind him with a loaded gun,
at seven use an axe . . . drive his Ford car
anywhere at twelve . . . My freedom was complete,
all he asked for was responsibility in turn.

—*Charles A. Lindbergh Jr.*

KNIGHTS IN SHINING ARMOR
Fathers

My father gave me a trumpet because he
loved my mother so much.

—Miles Davis

There is a man in my house
He's so big and strong
He goes to work each day and stays all day long
Comes home at night, looking tired and beat
I think I'll color him Father . . .
I think I'll color him love.

—O. C. Smith

Dad and I have things to teach [to] and learn
from each other in eternity. That should be
just about enough time.

—Fred Rogers (Mr. Rogers)

Just a little flash like the gesture of my hand
in a conversation and WHAM, there's my
old man. Right there, living inside me
like a worm in the wood.

—Sam Shepard

I talk and talk and talk, and I haven't taught
people in fifty years what my father taught
me by example in one week.

—Mario Cuomo

Fathers

I never put aside
the past resentment of the boy
until, with my own sons, I shared
his final hours, and came to see
what he'd become, or always was—
the father who will never cease to be
alive in me.

—Jimmy Carter

My father is my idol, so I always did
everything like him.

—Earvin (Magic) Johnson

With him, every day was an adventure. It was like my dad and I were buddies, and there was no real sorrow then.

—*Sean Lennon*

How lucky I was to have a father, who, in spite of formidable obstacles, would fight for his beliefs and ambitions and win!

—*Benjamin Davis Jr.*

There are those who say they never really knew their father very well, and to them I say I am truly sorry.

—*Osgood Perkins*

I shall never forget my mother's horror and my father's cry of joy when, for the first time in my life, I said angrily to my father, 'That's not the hand I dealt you, Dad.'

—*J. B. Morton*

My mother taught me my ABCs. From my father I learned the glories of going to the bathroom outside.

—*Lewis Grizzard*

My dad was determined that if I wanted to,
I would become a baseball player and not end
up in the steel mills the way he did.

—*Willie Mays*

Knights in shining armor . . . Fathers in
shining trousers . . . there's little difference . . .
As they march away to work each workday.

—*Paul Harvey*

My mother was like a drill sergeant.
Dad was the commanding general . . .

—*George Bush*

Sundays too my father got up early
and put his clothes on in the blueblack cold,
then with cracked hands that ached
from labor in the weekday weather made
banked fire blazes. No one ever thanked him.

—*Robert Hayden*

The man my brother knew as a father was not the
same one I'd known. People change—even fathers.

—*Leo Buscaglia*

If I had one wish for something that would give me personal joy and satisfaction, it would be to have my father come back and show him around. I'd like to show him the whole shooting match.

—*Ted Turner*

My father would have enjoyed what you have so generously said of me—and my mother would have believed it.

—*Lyndon B. Johnson*

It was only in that moment that I realized how much I really loved him and needed him and that I had never told him.

—*Humphrey Bogart*

PART JOY AND PART GUERRILLA WARFARE

Parenting

The thing that impresses me most about America
is the way the parents obey their children.

—the Duke of Windsor

Happy is the father whose child finds his
attempts to amuse it amusing.

—Robert Lynd

Should a father be present at the birth of
his child? It's all any reasonable child can
expect if dad is present at the conception.

—Joe Orton

The best time of my life has been the three instances where I have been there for the birth of my children. That is, nothing [else] has ever come close.

—*Steven Spielberg*

It's the practice of parenthood that makes you feel that, after all, there may be something in it.

—*Heywood C. Broun*

No matter how calmly you try to referee, parenting will eventually produce bizarre behavior, and I'm not talking about the kids. Their behavior is always normal.

—*Bill Cosby*

Like any father, I have moments when
I wonder whether I belong to my children
or they belong to me.

—*Bob Hope*

As a father of two
there is a respectful question
which I wish to ask of fathers of five:
How do you happen to be still alive?

—*Ogden Nash*

Anyone who hasn't had children
doesn't know what life is.

—*Henry Miller*

No man can possibly know what life means,
what the world means, what anything means,
until he has a child and loves it.

—Lafcadio Hearn

We never know the love of our parent for us
till we have become parents.

—Henry Ward Beecher

It is my hope that my son, when I am gone,
will remember me not from the battle but
in the home repeating with him our
simple daily prayer . . .

—General Douglas MacArthur

I have always been careful about giving
[my children] money. They wanted for nothing;
but they were taught not to want too much.

—*General Colin Powell*

Rediscovering fatherhood a second time, I was
finding that like youth, it is wasted on the young.

—*Arthur Miller*

He may be President, but he still
comes home and steals my socks!

—*Joseph P. Kennedy*

It is our continuing love for our children
that makes us want them to become all they
can be, and their continuing love for us helps
them accept healthy discipline—from us and
eventually from themselves.

—*Fred Rogers (Mr. Rogers)*

How can you say no to a child?
How can one be anything but a slave to one's
own flesh and blood?

—*Henry Miller*

Nothing you do for children is ever wasted.
They seem not to notice us, hovering, averting
our eyes, and they seldom offer thanks, but
what we do for them is never wasted.

—*Garrison Keillor*

There are only two lasting bequests we
can hope to give our children.
One of these is roots; the other, wings.

—*Hodding Carter*

• • • What you do for yourselves and for your
children can never be taken away.

—*Robert F. Kennedy*

In spite of the six thousand manuals on child raising in the bookstores, child raising is still a dark continent and no one really knows anything. You just need a lot of love and luck—and, of course, courage.

—*Bill Cosby*

Raising kids is part joy and part guerrilla warfare.

—*Edward Asner*

Age seventeen is the point in the journey when
the parents retire to the observation car . . .
when you stop being critical of your eldest son
and he starts being critical of you.

—James B. Reston

Having one child makes you a parent; having
two you are a referee.

—David Frost

Parenthood remains the greatest single
preserve of the amateur.

—Alvin Toffler

What the best and wisest parent wants for his own child, that must be what the community wants for all its children.

—John Dewey

Everyone likes to think that he has done reasonably well in life, so that it comes as a shock to find out our children believing differently. The temptation is to tune them out; it takes much more courage to listen.

—John D. Rockefeller III

There are times when parenthood seems nothing but feeding the mouth that bites you.

—Peter De Vries

Parents give you advice and never stop to think
of what you think of what they turned out to be.

—Harold Brodkey

. . . little by little the American father has
become established on the television screen as
Nature's last word in saps, boobs and total
losses, the man with two left feet who can't move
in any direction without falling over himself.

—P. G. Wodehouse

A child prodigy is one with highly
imaginative parents.

—Will Rogers

Curly, Dimpled Lunatics

Children

Children

A child is a curly, dimpled lunatic.

—Ralph Waldo Emerson

Childhood is to youth what manhood is to age.

—Herman Melville

Children are not our creations but our guests.

—John Updike

Children have never been very good at
listening to their elders, but they have never
failed to imitate them.

—*James Baldwin*

All kids need is a little help, a little hope,
and somebody who believes in them.

—*Earvin (Magic) Johnson*

Every day American children throw over
sixteen pounds of french fries at perfectly
innocent customers while screaming,
'Daddy, look at that monster lady.'

—*Hugh O'Neill*

That energy which makes a child hard to
manage is the energy which afterward
makes him a manager of life.

—*Henry Ward Beecher*

. . . the most used word in a child's
dictionary is 'why?'

—*Steven Spielberg*

A child is a quicksilver fountain
Spilling over with tomorrows and tomorrows
And that is why
She is richer than you or I.

—*Tom Bradley*

There isn't a child who hasn't gone out
into the brave new world who eventually
doesn't return to the old homestead
carrying a bundle of dirty clothes.

—*Art Buchwald*

We mold the views of our children from
their earliest days in many ways, some open,
some subtle. Long after they are gone from
the home these views remain with them,
some as haunting as a demon.

—*Bob Keeshan (Captain Kangaroo)*

Water fascinates kids. They run toward it, and
they run away from it. They love it in a lake or
an ocean, but it's a necessary evil in a bathtub.

—*Art Linkletter*

Adolescence is that period in a kid's life when
his or her parents become more difficult.

—Ryan O'Neal

Life affords no greater responsibility,
no greater privilege, than the raising of
the next generation.

—C. Everett Koop

I have learned that my kids, like most kids,
would rather work all night long in a salt
mine than rake leaves at home.

—Phil Donahue

Children

A child's spirit is like a child, you can never catch it by running after it; you must stand still, and, for love, it will soon itself come back.

—*Arthur Miller*

We've had bad luck with our kids— they've all grown up.

—*Christopher Morley*

A child becomes an adult when he realizes that he has a right not only to be right, but also to be wrong.

—*Thomas Szasz*

A child miseducated is a child lost.

—*John F. Kennedy*

Really give yourself to your children just as your parents gave themselves to you because they are the future of your generation.

—*Ross Perot*

Children are a great investment. They beat the hell out of stocks.

—*Peter Lynch*

Where children are concerned, I never believed that possessions could buy love, popularity, respect or accomplishment.

—*General Colin Powell*

I confess pride in the coming generation. You
are working out your own salvation; you are more
in love with life; you play with fire openly, where
we did in secret, and few of you are burned.

—*Franklin D. Roosevelt*

A child is a person who is going to carry
on what you have started . . . that fate of
humanity is in his hands.

—*Abraham Lincoln*

Youth comes but once in a lifetime.

—*Henry Wadsworth Longfellow*

If youth is a defect, it is one that we
outgrow too soon.

—*Robert Lowell*

Youth is the turning point of life, the
most sensitive and volatile period, the state
that registers most vividly the impressions
and experience of life.

—*Richard Wright*

We will die without our young people.

—*Alex Haley*

Each child is an adventure into a better life—
an opportunity to change the old pattern
and make it new.

—*Hubert H. Humphrey*

If all the world thought and acted like children,
we'd never have any trouble. The only pity is
even kids have to grow up.

—*Walt Disney*

It is easier to build strong children than to
repair broken men.

—*Frederick Douglass*

The reconstruction of children is more
precious than factories and bridges.

—*Herbert Hoover*

A torn jacket is soon mended, but hard words
bruise the heart of a child.

—Henry Wadsworth Longfellow

What's done to children, they will do to society.

—Karl Menninger

A person's a person no matter how small.

—Theodor Geisel (Dr. Seuss)

We find delight in the beauty and happiness of
children that makes the heart too big for the body.

—Ralph Waldo Emerson

THE STEADY ROCK
Family

Never come between blood and blood.

—Clint Eastwood

. . . We may find some of our best friends
in our own blood.

—Ralph Waldo Emerson

The only rock I know that stays steady, the only
institution I know that works, is the family.

—Lee Iacocca

Other things may change us, but we start
and end with the family.

—*Anthony Brandt*

The happiest moments of my life have been
the few which I have passed at home in the
bosom of my family.

—*Thomas Jefferson*

For unflagging interest and enjoyment, a household of children, if things go reasonably well, certainly makes all other forms of success and achievement lose their importance by comparison.

—Theodore Roosevelt

No one on his deathbed ever said, 'I wish I had spent more time on my business.'

—Paul Tsongas

The family you come from isn't as important as the family you're going to have.

—Ring Lardner

[In a big family] the first child is kind of like
the first pancake. If it's not perfect, that's okay,
there are a lot more coming along.

—Antonin Scalia

When you're the only pea in the pod,
your parents are likely to get you confused
with the Hope diamond.

—Russell Baker

I was the seventh of nine children, and
when you come from that far down you
have to struggle to survive.

—Robert F. Kennedy

Every family has a secret, and the secret is
that it's not like other families.

—*Alan Bennett*

Family life is the basis for a strong
community and a great nation.

—*Bing Crosby*

Homesick is a queer word as we use it
sometimes when what we really mean is that we
would like to be in two places at the same time.
And so we are trying to live more of life than
can be lived in one place at a certain time.

—*Carl Sandburg*

Home is the sanctuary where the healing is . . .

—*Walter Cronkite*

Home is the place there's no place like.

—*Charles Schulz*

There is nothing emptier than a house once occupied by a wife and five children . . .

—*Phil Donahue*

Happiness is having a large, loving, caring close-knit family in another city.

—*George Burns*

Families break up when people take hints you don't intend and miss hints you do intend.

—*Robert Frost*

New Tremors from Old Earthquakes
Life Lessons

If there must be trouble let it be in my day,
that my child may have peace.

—*Thomas Paine*

I know there is no good in my trying to explain
to you why I am away from home—war doesn't
make any sense even when you are grown up.

—*(Lieutenant) Henry Fonda*

May you build a ladder to the stars
and climb on every rung.
And, may you stay forever young.

—*Bob Dylan*

When we leave our child in nursery school for
the first time, it won't be just our child's feelings
about separation that we will have to cope with,
but our own feelings as well—from our present
and from our past, parents are extra vulnerable
to new tremors from old earthquakes.

—*Fred Rogers (Mr. Rogers)*

One of the most painful experiences I have ever faced was to see [my daughter's] tears when I told her that Funtown was closed to colored children . . . for at that moment the first dark cloud . . . had floated into her little mental sky.

—Martin Luther King Jr.

. . . We all fear the unknown—the strange, the different. The natural fears of parents are made worse by ignorance, and unfortunately, they pass them down to their children.

—Jackie Robinson

I have a dream . . . that my four little children will one day live in a nation where they will not be judged by the color of their skin but by the content of their character.

—Martin Luther King Jr.

. . . Never follow anybody who's working less than you.

—Ellis Marsalis

You can make it. It gets dark sometimes, but
the morning comes. Don't you surrender.
Suffering breeds character. Character breeds
faith. In the end, faith will not disappoint.

—Jesse Jackson

All I believe in in life is the rewards for
virtue (according to your talents) and the
punishments for not fulfilling your duties,
which are doubly costly.

—F. Scott Fitzgerald

You'll make a lot of mistakes in your life . . .
but if you learn from every mistake,
you really didn't make a mistake.

—Vince Lombardi

Son, sometimes no action is action.
The army that marches forward is not
always the one that wins.

—*Ellis Marsalis*

Son, you get out of it what you put into it.

—*Earl Woods*

As you journey through [life], you will
encounter all sorts of these nasty little upsets,
and you will either learn to adjust yourself
to them or gradually go nuts.

—*Groucho Marx*

In the really important decisions of life, others
cannot help you. No matter how much they
would like to. You must rely only on yourself.
That is the fate of each one of us.

—Eugene O'Neill

You don't want to do what I'm doing.

—Vince Lombardi

You have everything to live for.
Put yourself in condition to live.

—William Randolph Hearst

WISDOM WITH BUBBLE GUM IN ITS HAIR

Sons and Daughters

. . . When we had a girl, all of a sudden
I couldn't remember that I ever wanted
to have a boy.

—*Henry Louis Gates Jr.*

She entered the world with a commanding
voice and has been taking over ever since.

—*Lyndon B. Johnson*

When you were a few weeks old, you smiled
on us. I sometimes see the same look and the
same smile on your face, and feel that my
daughter is yet good and pure. O keep it there,
my daughter, and never lose it.

—*Bronson Alcott*

I only have two rules for my newly born
daughter: she will dress well and never have sex.

—*John Malkovich*

Past experience indicates that the best way of
dealing with her is total attention and love.

—*Lyndon B. Johnson*

It wasn't until she was two and realized she was
stuck with me that she said, during a walk
through autumn leaves, 'I love you . . .'

—*James Thurber*

Not love me, eh? She better had!
By Jove, I'll make her love me one day;
For, don't you see, I am her Dad,
And she'll be three weeks old on Sunday.

—*Christopher Morley*

Many a man wishes he were strong enough
to tear a telephone book in half—especially
if he has a teenage daughter.

—*Guy Lombardo*

Then farewell, my dear;
my loved daughter, adieu,
The last pang of life is in parting from you.

—*Thomas Jefferson*

It isn't that I'm a weak father,
it's just that she's a strong daughter.

—*Henry Fonda*

The meaningful role of the father of the bride
was played out long before the church music
began. It stretched across those years of infancy
and puberty, adolescence and young adulthood.
That's when she needs you at her side.

—*Tom Brokaw*

The other night, my little teenage daughter
came home and said—and I don't think she was
being very original—'Daddy, as an outsider,
how do you feel about the human race?'

—*Lyndon B. Johnson*

. . . little girls are in fact smaller versions of
real human beings, whereas little boys are Pod
People from the Planet Destructo.

—*Dave Barry*

Boyhood is the natural state of rascality.

—*Herman Melville*

A boy is Truth with dirt on its face,
Beauty with a cut on its finger,
Wisdom with bubble gum in its hair and
Hope of the future with a frog in its pocket.

—*Alan Beck*

He makes fuzz come out of my bald patch!

—Charles A. Lindbergh Jr.

There are to us no ties at all in just being a father. A son is distinctly an acquired taste.

—Heywood C. Broun

The father is always a Republican toward his son, and his mother's always a Democrat.

—Robert Frost

If you've never seen a real, fully-developed look of disgust, tell your son how you conducted yourself when you were a boy.

—Kin Hubbard

A boy wants something very special from his father. You hear it said that fathers want their sons to be what they feel they cannot themselves be, but I tell you it also works the other way.

—*Sherwood Anderson*

Helping your eldest son pick a college is one of the great educational experiences of life . . . Next to trying to pick his bride, it's the best way to learn that your authority, if not entirely gone, is slipping fast.

—*James B. Reston*

Every son, at one point or another, defies
his father, fights him, departs from him, only
to return to him—if he is lucky—closer and
more secure than before.

—*Leonard Bernstein*

The use of a university is to make young
gentlemen as unlike their fathers as possible.

—*Woodrow Wilson*

In my younger and more vulnerable years, my
father gave me some advice I've been turning
over in my mind ever since.

—*F. Scott Fitzgerald*

We must make our boys understand the
difference between making a baby
and being a father.

—*William Raspberry*

Would that all son's fathers were poets! For the
poem and the world are the same.

—*Allen Ginsberg*

A father follows the course of his son's life
and notes many things of which he has not
the privilege to speak. He sees, of course, his
own past life unfolding . . .

—*William Carlos Williams*

Fatherlessness is the most destructive trend of
our generation.

—*David Blankenhorn*

I am not a chip off the old block, I am 'the
block itself,' living again, a reincarnation.

—*Adam Clayton Powell Jr.*

Masculinity is not something given to you, but something you gain. And you gain it by winning small battles with your honor.

—*Norman Mailer*

Build me a son, O Lord, who will be strong enough to know when he is weak, and brave enough to face himself when he is afraid; one who will be proud and unbending in honest defeat, and humble and gentle in victory.

—*General Douglas MacArthur*

It's a wonderful feeling when your father becomes not a god but a man to you. When he comes down from the mountain and you see he's this man with weaknesses. And you love him as a whole being, not as a figurehead.

—*Robin Williams*

SHUTTLES ON A LOOM
The Joys of Parenting

There is no friendship, no love, like that of
the parent for the child.

—Henry Ward Beecher

The affection of a parent for his child is never
permitted to die.

—James Fenimore Cooper

A father's interest in having a child—
perhaps his only child—may be unmatched by
any other interest in his life.

—William Rehnquist

If you are the first child, you are one of two
most amazing things that happened to your
parents. A couple. And if you came later in the
family, you were just as amazing as that, but
without all of the worry and the facts.

—*Garrison Keillor*

Children make you want to start life over.

—*Muhammad Ali*

When you become a parent it is your
biggest chance to grow again. You have
another crack at yourself.

—*Fred Rogers (Mr. Rogers)*

. . . You will judge yourself by how your
children turn out.

—Ross Perot

Blessings on thee, little man
Barefoot boy, with cheek of tan! . . .
From my heart I give thee joy—
I was once a barefoot boy!

—John Greenleaf Whittier

By profession I am a soldier and take pride in
that fact. But I am prouder—infinitely prouder—
to be a father.

—General Douglas MacArthur

Every one of your letters I read first for the
facts and the fun—and then a second time to see
how the red inside heart of you is ticking.

—*Carl Sandburg*

Who shall say I am not,
the happy genius of my household?

—*William Carlos Williams*

I'm really profoundly proud and fond of you—
after my fashion which is inarticulate about such
things—and I know there is a rare feeling
between us that ought to make both of our
lives richer as years go by.

—*Eugene O'Neill*

I feel blessed, but quite frankly . . .
I used to say 'Why me, Lord? What have I done
to deserve this beautiful and special kid?'

—*Earl Woods*

Parents are like shuttles on a loom. They join
the threads of the past with threads of the future
and leave their own bright patterns as they go.

—*Fred Rogers (Mr. Rogers)*

By the time the youngest children have learned to keep the house tidy, the oldest grandchildren are on hand to tear it to pieces.

—*Christopher Morley*

Nobody can do for little children what grandparents do. Grandparents sort of sprinkle stardust over the lives of little children.

—*Alex Haley*

There is nothing like having grandchildren to restore your faith in heredity.

—*Doug Larson*

Because [grandparents] are usually free to love
and guide and befriend the young without
having to take daily responsibility for them, they
can often reach out past pride and fear of
failure and close the space between generations.

—*Jimmy Carter*

Few things seem more satisfying than seeing
your children have teenagers of their own.

—*Doug Larson*

Posterity is the patriotic name for grandchildren.

—*Art Linkletter*

If the Very Old Remember
Teachings

Youth are looking for something; it's up to
adults to show them what is worth emulating.

—*Jesse Jackson*

We cannot always build the future for our youth,
but we can build our youth for the future.

—*Franklin D. Roosevelt*

Make a world worthy of the children
your generation will bear.

—*Carl Sagan*

Learn about your family. Find out about your grandmother's grandfather. Where was he in 1861? It will help you, I promise.

—*Ken Burns*

It seems to be typical of life in America, where opportunities, real and fancied, are thicker than anywhere else on the globe, that the second generation has no time to talk to the first.

—*James Baldwin*

Setting a good example for your children takes all the fun out of middle age.

—*William Feather*

Anybody who is in a position to discipline others should first learn to accept discipline himself.

—*Malcolm X*

Discipline itself must be disciplined.

—*M. Scott Peck*

If you take care of yourself and your family and provide that one unit of well-being in the world, you'll have done your part.

—*Andy Rooney*

Every adult is a teacher to every child.

—*Dan Rather*

Millions of Americans, especially our own sons and daughters, are seeking a cause they can believe in. There is a hunger in the country today—a hunger for spiritual guidance.

—*Ronald Reagan*

Your parents left you a perfect world. Don't louse it up.

—*Art Buchwald*

Once you bring life into the world, you must protect it. We must protect it by changing the world.

—*Elie Wiesel*

If the very old will remember,
the very young will listen.

—*Chief Dan George*

If I were given the opportunity to present a gift
to the next generation, it would be the ability
for each individual to learn to laugh at himself.

—*Charles Schulz*

There is a 'sanctity' involved with bringing
a child into this world; it is better than
bombing one out of it.

—*James Baldwin*

Do not neglect your work, but start families.
Make babies, lots of them. Say twenty-five.

—*Ken Burns*

If men do not keep on speaking terms with
children, they cease to be men, and become
merely machines for eating and for earning money.

—*John Updike*

Perhaps a child who is fussed over gets a
feeling of destiny, he thinks he is in the
world for something important and it
gives him drive and confidence.

—Benjamin Spock

My parents were constantly affirming me in
everything I did. Late at night I'd wake up
and hear my mother talking over my bed,
saying, 'You're going to do great on this test.
You can do anything you want.'

—Stephen Covey

The point I want to make to you is, role models can be black. Role models can be white. Role models can be generals. Role models can be principals, teachers, doctors, or just your parent who brought you into this world and who is trying to give you the best of everything.

—*General Colin Powell*

You need a lot of money to raise a
modern child. Hair gel alone will run
you thousands of dollars.

—*Dave Barry*

What maintains one Vice would bring
up two children.

—*Benjamin Franklin*

I have found the best way to give advice to
your children is to find out what they want
and then advise them to do it.

—*Harry S. Truman*

If you want to recapture your youth,
cut off his allowance.

—*Al Bernstein*

The child supplies the power, but the parents
do the steering.

—*Benjamin Spock*

As you raise your families, remember the
worst kind of poverty is not economic poverty,
it is the poverty of values. It is the poverty of
caring. It is the poverty of love.

—*General Colin Powell*

Some authority on parenting once said,
'Hold them very close and then let them go.'
This is the hardest truth for a father to learn:
that his children are continuously growing up
and moving away from him . . .

—*Bill Cosby*

If we suffer their minds to grovel and creep
in infancy, they will grovel all their lives.

—*John Adams*

As our children grow, so must we grow to
meet their changing emotional, intellectual,
and designer-footwear needs.

—*Dave Barry*

Sometimes you struggle so hard to feed your
family one way, you forget to feed them the
other way, with spiritual nourishment.
Everybody needs that.

—James Brown

Kennedys don't cry.

—John F. Kennedy

If a man smiles at home somebody is
sure to ask for money.

—William Feather

If the Very Old Remember Teachings

At its best, parenting occurs in the spirit of equal partnership.

—*Benjamin Spock*

RESPECT THE CHILD

Advice to Parents

There are one hundred and fifty-two
distinctly different ways of holding a baby—
and all are right.

—*Heywood C. Broun*

When you're drawing up your list of life's
miracles, you might place near the top the first
moment your baby smiles at you.

—*Bob Greene*

Never will a time come when the most
marvelous recent invention is as marvelous
as a newborn baby.

—*Carl Sandburg*

People who say they sleep like a baby usually
don't have one.

—*Leo J. Burke*

I love to think that the day you're born, you're
given the world as a birthday present.

—*Leo Buscaglia*

Infancy is the perpetual Messiah, which comes into the arms of fallen men, and pleads with them to return to paradise.

—*Ralph Waldo Emerson*

The first cry of a newborn baby in Chicago or Zamboango, in Amsterdam or Rangoon, has the same pitch and key, each saying 'I am! I have come through! I belong!'

—*Carl Sandburg*

Taking care of a newborn baby means devoting
yourself, body and soul, twenty-four hours
a day, seven days a week, to the welfare of
someone whose major response, in the way of
positive reinforcement, is to throw up on you.

—*Dave Barry*

A baby is God's opinion that life should go on.

—*Carl Sandburg*

A good father is a little bit of a mother.

—*Lee Salk*

When a child can be brought to tears, not from fear of punishment, but from repentance for his offense, he needs no chastisement. When the tears begin to flow from grief at one's own conduct, be sure there is an angel nestling in the bosom.

—*Horace Mann*

Babies are always more trouble than you
thought—and more wonderful.

—*Charles Osgood*

Parents should sit tall in the saddle and look
upon their troops with a noble and benevolent
and extremely near-sighted gaze.

—*Garrison Keillor*

The most important thing parents can teach
their children is how to get along without them.

—*Frank Clark*

Try to see your children as whole and complete . . .
as though they are already what they can become.

—*Wayne Dyer*

Respect the child. Be not too much his parent.
Trespass not on his solitude.

—*Ralph Waldo Emerson*

Let your children go if you want to keep them.

—*Malcolm Forbes*

Trust yourself.
You know more than you think you do.

—*Benjamin Spock*

Children will send verbal and non-verbal
signals when everything is not okay.
Parents have but to listen.

—*Bob Keeshan (Captain Kangaroo)*

The baby whose cries are answered now will
later be the child confident enough to show his
independence and curiosity.

—*Lee Salk*

Let thy child's first lesson be obedience,
and the second will be what thou wilt.

—*Benjamin Franklin*

Our only realistic hope, as I see it, is first to bring up our children with a feeling that they are in this world not for their own satisfaction but primarily to serve others.

—Benjamin Spock

Re: raising kids: Love, without discipline, isn't.

—Malcolm Forbes

The most important thing in the world is that you make yourself the greatest, grandest, most wonderful loving person in the world because this is what you are going to be giving to your children . . .

—*Leo Buscaglia*

Your children need your presence more than
your presence.

—Jesse Jackson

It should be your care, therefore,
and mine, to elevate the minds of our
children and exalt their courage . . .

—John Adams

Better to play fifteen minutes enjoyably and
then say, 'Now I'm going to read my paper' than
to spend all day at the zoo crossly.

—Benjamin Spock

TOLERATE YOUR PARENTS
Advice to Children

Always obey your parents, when they
are present.

—*Mark Twain*

Try to remain humble.
Smartness kills everything.

—*Sherwood Anderson*

Be smart, but never show it.

—*L. B. Mayer*

Where there is no occasion for expressing an
opinion, it is best to be silent . . .

—*George Washington*

I don't want you to be a soldier or a priest but a
good useful man.

—*William Tecumseh Sherman*

Next [in importance] to occupation is the
building up of good taste. That is difficult,
slow work. Few achieve it. It means all the
difference in the world.

—*Sherwood Anderson*

. . . a man might do some might good work
and not be a gentleman in any sense.

—*Theodore Roosevelt*

After all, parents' advice is no damned good.
You know that as well as I. The best I can do is
try to encourage you to work hard at something
you really want to do and have the ability to do.

—*Eugene O'Neill*

From this dear children you should sense
The value of obedience.
When I say 'Don't,' I mean 'Postpone'
Some naughtiness for when you're grown . . .

—*Garrison Keillor*

Keep your balance, the grades don't matter.

—Robert Frost

You know what makes a good loser? Practice.

—Ernest Hemingway

Girls have a way of knowing or feeling what you feel, but they usually like to hear it also.

—John Steinbeck

Think the best of people, do not dwell upon
their faults, [and] try not to see them.
You will be happier for it.

—*Mark Twain*

It's important to be smart in school, but it's
even more important to be smart about yourself.

—*Irving Berlin*

Tolerating your parents . . . will soon give
way to the even more challenging occupation
of tolerating your children.

—*Alistair Cooke*

You'll have many, many friends, but if your relationship with your mate is one hundred percent of your heart, you'll never need a friend.

—*Bill Cosby*

Marriage is our last, best chance to grow up.

—*Joseph Barth*

The value of marriage is not that adults produce children but that children produce adults.

—*Peter De Vries*

Where there is marriage without love, there will be love without marriage.

—*Benjamin Franklin*

The most important thing a father can do for his children is to love their mother.

—Reverend Theodore Hesburgh

Harmony in the marriage state is the very first object to be aimed at.

—Thomas Jefferson

Rituals are important. Nowadays its hip not to be married. I'm not interested in being hip.

—John Lennon

We have many things in common the greatest of which is that we are both afraid of children.

—Bill Cosby

Married life requires shared mystery even
when all the facts are known.

—Richard Ford

It sometimes happens that what you feel is
not returned for one reason or another—
but that does not make your feeling less
valuable and good.

—John Steinbeck

Parental love is the only real charity going.
It never comes back. A one-way street.

—*Abbie Hoffman*

You don't have to deserve your mother's love.
You have to deserve your father's.
He's more particular.

—*Robert Frost*

Next to God, thy parents.

—*William Penn*

The object of love is the best and most
beautiful. Try to live up to it.

—*John Steinbeck*

EXPLORE, DREAM, DISCOVER

The Journey of Life

Man's main task in his life is to give
birth to himself.

—Eric Fromm

. . . Every generation revolts against its
fathers and makes friend with its grandfathers.

—Lewis Mumford

Circumstances have nothing to do with
success. When you have made up your
mind, success is certain.

—William Randolph Hearst

It isn't your success I want. There is a possibility of your having a decent attitude toward people and work. That alone may make a man of you.

—*Sherwood Anderson*

Where creative effort is involved, there are no trivial circumstances. The most trivial of them may ruin the whole issue.

—*Frank Lloyd Wright*

All the performances of human art, at which we look with praise or wonder, are instances of the resistless force of perseverance.

—*Samuel Johnson*

Character, not circumstances, make the man.

—*Booker T. Washington*

The heights by great men reached and kept
Were not attained by sudden flight,
But they, while their companions slept,
Were toiling upward in the night.

—*Henry Wadsworth Longfellow*

I learned from my father how to work.
I learned from him that work is life and life
is work, and work is hard.

—*Philip Roth*

He who is taught to live upon little owes more to his father's wisdom than he who has a great deal left him does to his father's care.

—*William Penn*

You can't escape the responsibility of tomorrow by evading it today.

—*Abraham Lincoln*

The most important thing for a young man is to establish credit—a reputation, character.

—*John D. Rockefeller*

• • • good name and honor are worth more than all the gold and jewels ever mined.

—*Harry S. Truman*

You must keep your mind on the objective,
not on the obstacle.

—*William Randolph Hearst*

The parent who leaves his son enormous
wealth generally deadens the talents
and energies of the son.

—*Andrew Carnegie*

Wise people who save money have just as much satisfaction out of savings as jackasses have out of spending it.

—*William Randolph Hearst*

Twenty years from now you will be more disappointed by the things you didn't do than by the ones you did do. So throw off the bowlines. Sail away from the safe harbor. Catch the trade winds in your sails. Explore. Dream. Discover.

—*Mark Twain*

For everything you have missed you have
gained something else.

—*Ralph Waldo Emerson*

Try not to be a man of success but rather
a man of value.

—*Albert Einstein*

Your dad will never be reckoned among
the great. But you can be sure he did his level
best and gave all he had to his country . . .
What more can a person do?

—*Harry S. Truman*

Walking on water wasn't built in a day.

—*Jack Kerouac*

Any given generation gives the next generation advice that the given generation should have been given by the previous one but now it's too late.

—*Ray Blount Jr.*

EXPLORE, DREAM, DISCOVER
The Journey of Life

Our first youth is of no value; for we are never
conscious of it, until after it is gone.
—*Nathaniel Hawthorne*

My dad told me there's no difference between
a black snake and a white snake. They both bite.
—*Thurgood Marshall*

Honor does not descend, but ascend.
—*Benjamin Franklin*

Always remember life is not as complex as
many people would have you think.
—*Thomas Watson Sr.*

All men have faults. Small men are blind to their own, and therefore remain small.

—*Jean Toomer*

. . . Character counts for a great deal more than either intellect or body in winning success in life . . .

—*Theodore Roosevelt*

. . . It is so remarkably easy just to tell the truth in this world, that I often marvel that there are so many madly foolish, so wretchedly stupid, that they hide truth.

—*Jack London*

Life is a problem in virtual velocity.
The purpose . . . is the direction.

—William Tecumseh Sherman

When I was a boy of fourteen, my father was so
ignorant, I could hardly stand to have the old
man around. But when I got to be twenty-one,
I was astonished at how much the old man
had learned in seven years.

—Mark Twain

You won't arrive. It is an endless search.

—Sherwood Anderson

Index

Index

Index

BIBLIOGRAPHY

Adler, Bill, ed. *Presidential Wit From Washington to Johnson.* New York: Trident Press, 1996.

Albanese, Andrew and Brandon Trissler, eds. *Graduation Day.* New York: William Morrow, 1998.

Ali, Muhammad. *The Greatest.* New York: Ballantine Books, 1975.

Andrews, Robert, ed. *Famous Lines: A Columbia Dictionary of Familiar Quotations.* New York: Columbia University Press, 1996.

Baker, Russell. *Inventing the Truth: The Art and Craft of Memoir.* Edited by William Zinsser. Boston: Houghton Mifflin, 1987.

Baldwin, James. *Nobody Knows My Name: More Notes of a Native Son.* New York: Dell Publishing Company, 1961.

Barrett, Mary Ellin. *Irving Berlin: A Daughter's Memoir.* New York: Simon & Schuster, 1994.

Barry, Dave. *Dave Barry Turns 40.* New York: Crown, 1990.

Bedell, Madelon. *The Alcotts: Biography of a Family.* New York: Clarkson Potter, 1980.

Beecher, Henry Ward. *Proverbs from Plymouth Pulpit,* 1887.

Bell, Janet Cheatham, ed. *The Soul of Success: Inspiring Quotations.* New York: J. Wiley, 1997.

Bennett, Alan. *Writing Home.* New York: Random House, 1994.

Bennett, William J., ed. *Our Sacred Honor.* New York: Simon & Schuster, 1997.

Berg, Scott A. *Lindbergh.* New York: G. P. Putnam's, 1998.

Bernstein, Burton. *Thurber, A Biography.* New York: Dodd, Mead, 1975.

Bishop, Joseph Bucklin, ed. *Theodore Roosevelt's Letters to His Children.* New York: Scribner's, 1919.

Blankenhorn, David. *Fatherless America.* New York: Basic Books, 1995.

Bogart, Stephen Humphrey. *Bogart: In Search of My Father.* New York: Dutton, 1995.

BIBLIOGRAPHY

Bohle, Bruce, ed. *The Home Book of American Quotations.* New York: Dodd, 1967.

Brallier, Jess M., ed. *Presidential Wit & Wisdom: Maxims, Mottoes, Sound Bites, Speeches, and Asides.* New York: Penguin Books, 1996.

Braude, Jacob Morton, ed. *Lifetime Speaker's Encyclopedia.* Englewood Cliffs, NJ: Prentice Hall, 1962.

Brodkey, Harold. *First Love and Other Sorrows.* New York: Dial Press, 1957.

Broun, Heywood C. *Pieces of Hate and Other Enthusiasms.* New York: George H. Doran, 1922.

Brown, James and Bruce Tucker. *The Godfather of Soul.* New York: Macmillan, 1986.

Broyard, Anatole. *Aroused by Books.* New York: Random House, 1974.

Burton, Humphrey. *Leonard Bernstein.* Garden City, NY: Doubleday, 1994.

Buscaglia, Leo. *Papa, My Father: A Celebration of Dads.* Thorofare, NJ: Slack, 1989.

Butterfield, L. H., March Friedlaender, and Mary-Jo Kline, eds. *The Book of Abigail and John: Selected Letters of the Adams Family, 1762–1884.* Cambridge, MA: Harvard University Press and Massachussetts Historical Society, 1975.

Byrne, Robert and Teressa Skelton. *Every Day is Father's Day: The Best Things Ever Said About Dear Old Dad.* New York: Macmillan, 1989.

Camp, Wesley D., ed. *What a Piece of Work Is Man! Camp's Unfamiliar Quotations From 2000 B.C. to the Present.* Englewood Cliffs, NJ: Prentice Hall, 1990.

Carruth, Gorton, ed. *Harper Book of American Quotations.* New York: Harper & Row, 1988.

Carter, Hodding. *Reader's Digest* (May 1953): 52.

Carter, Jimmy. *Always a Reckoning and Other Poems.* Thorndike, ME: G. K. Hall, 1995.

"Celebrities recall best advice given by their fathers." *Jet* 92 (1997): 56-62.

Cooper, James Fenimore. *The Last of the Mohicans.* New York: Books, Inc., 1896.

Cosby, Bill. *Fatherhood.* Garden City, NY: Doubleday, 1986

Davis, Merrell R. and William H. Gilman, eds. *The Letters of Herman Melville.* New Haven, CT: Yale University Press, 1960.

De Vries, Peter. *The Tunnel of Love.* Boston: Little, Brown, 1954.

Donado, Stephen, Joan Smith, Susan Mesher, and Rebecca Davidson, eds. *The New York Public Library Book of Twentieth-Century American Quotations.* New York: Stonesong Press Book, 1992.

Donahue, Phil. *Donahue, My Own Story.* New York: Simon & Schuster, 1979.

Douglas, Charles Noel, ed. *Forty Thousand Quotations, Prose and Poetical.* New York: G. Sully and Company, 1917.

Dylan, Bob. "Forever Young," from *Bob Dylan at Budokan.* Columbia Records, 1979.

Ehrlich, Eugene and Marshall DeBruhl, eds. *International Thesaurus of Quotations.* New York: Harper Perennial, 1996.

Eisel, Deborah Davis and Jill Swanson Reddig, eds. *Dictionary of Contemporary Quotations.* Syracuse, NY: John Gordan Burke Publisher, 1981.

Emerson, Ralph Waldo. *Hitch Your Wagon to a Star.* New York, Columbia University Press, 1996.

——. "Illusions," from *The Conduct of Life,* 1860.

——. *The Letters of Ralph Waldo Emerson,* volume six. Edited by Ralph L. Rusk. New York: Columbia University Press, 1939.

Ernst, Joseph W., ed. "Dear Father/Dear Son," *Correspondence of John D. Rockefeller and John D. Rockefeller Jr.* New York: Fordham University Press, 1994.

Feinstein, John. *A Season on the Brink: A Year with Bobby Knight and the Indiana Hoosiers.* New York: Simon & Schuster, 1986.

Fellman, Michael. *Citizen Sherman: A Life of William Tecumseh Sherman.* New York: Random House, 1995.

Fitzgerald, F. Scott. *The Great Gatsby.* New York: Charles Scribner's Sons, 1953.

Flynn, George L. *The Vince Lombardi Scrapbook.* New York: Grosset & Dunlap, 1976.

Fonda, Henry. *Fonda: My Life.* New York: New American Library, 1981.

Forbes Magazine, ed. *Thoughts on the Business of Life.* Chicago: Triumph Books, 1992.

Ford, Richard. *The Sportswriter.* New York: Vintage Books, 1986.

Freeman, Criswell, ed. *Fathers Are Forever.* Nashville: Walnut Grove Press, 1998.

Fromm, Eric. *Man for Himself.* New York: Rinehart, 1947.

Frost, Elizabeth, ed. *Bully Pulpit: Quotations From America's Presidents.* New York: Facts On File, 1988.

Frost, Robert and Elinor Frost. *Family Letters of Robert and Elinor Frost.* Edited by Arnold Grade. Albany, NY: State University of New York Press, 1972.

Ginsburg, Susan, ed. *Family Wisdom: The 2000 Most Important Things Ever Said About Parenting, Children and Family Life.* New York: Columbia University Press, 1996.

Goldberg, Robert and Gerald Jay Goldberg. *Citizen Turner.* New York: Harcourt Brace, 1995.

Goodman, Ted, ed. *Forbes Book of Business Quotations: 14,266 Thoughts on the Business of Life.* New York: Black Dog & Leventhal Publishers, 1997.

Green, Jonathon, comp. *Morrow's International Dictionary of Contemporary Quotations.* New York: William Morrow & Company, Inc., 1982.

Greene, Bob. *Good Morning, Merry Sunshine: A Father's Journal of His Child's First Year.* New York: Atheneum, 1984.

Griswold, Robert L., ed. *Fatherhood in America: A History.* New York: Basic Books, 1993.

Guinness, Louise, ed. *Fathers: An Anthology.* London: Random House, 1996.

Handley, Helen and Andra Samelson, eds. *Child*. Wainscott, NY: Pushcart Press, 1988.

Harnsbinger, Caroline. *Mark Twain, Family Man*. New York: Citadel Press, 1960.

Hawthorne, Nathaniel. *House of the Seven Gables*. London: W. Scott, 1893.

Hearst, William Randolph Jr. *The Hearsts, Father and Son*. New York: Roberts Rinehart, 1991.

Hemingway, Gregory H. *Papa: A Personal Memoir*. Boston: Houghton Mifflin, 1976.

Hill, Harold, ed. *Life Isn't Fair: 300 Years of Advice From History's Most Memorable Commencements*. New York: Berkley Publishing Group, 1997.

Hoffman, Edward. *The Book of Fathers' Wisdom: Paternal Advice from Moses to Bob Dylan*. Secaucus, NJ: Carol Publishing Group, 1998.

Iacocca, Lee and Sonny Kleinfeld. *Talking Straight*. Boston: G. K. Hall, 1988.

Jackson, Venice, ed. *Heart Full of Grace: A Thousand Years of Black Wisdom*. New York: Simon & Schuster, 1995.

Johnson, Magic and William Novak. *My Life*. New York: Random House, 1992.

Keeshan, Robert. *Growing Up Happy*. New York: Doubleday, 1989.

Keillor, Garrison. *The Book of Guys*. New York: Viking, 1993.

———. *Leaving Home*. New York: Viking, 1987.

———. *We Are Still Married*. New York: Viking, 1989.

Kennedy, Robert F. *Make Gentle the Life of This World: The Vision of Robert F. Kennedy*. New York: Harcourt Brace, 1998.

King, Martin Luther Jr. *The Autobiography of Martin Luther King Jr*. New York: Warner Books, 1998.

Levinson, Leonard Louis, ed. *Bartlett's Unfamiliar Quotations*. Chicago: Cowles Book Company, 1971.

London, Jack. *Letters from Jack London*. Edited by King Hendricks and Irving Shepard. New York: Odyssey, 1965.

Mailer, Norman. *Cannibals and Christians*. New York: Dial Press, 1966.

Martz, L. "A Pair for the Court." *Newsweek* 107 (June 30, 1986): 20-1.

Marx, Arthur. *My Life with Groucho: A Son's Eye View.* London: Robson Books, 1988.

Melville, Herman. *The Confidence Man.* New York: Airmont, 1966.

——. *Mardi and a Voyage Thither.* London: Constable and Company, Ltd., 1922.

Mencken, H. L., ed. *New Dictionary of Quotations on Historical Principles From Ancient and Modern Sources.* New York: Knopf, 1942.

Miller, Arthur. *Timebends: A Life.* New York: Grove Press, 1987.

Miller, Henry. *My Life and Times.* Chicago: Playboy Press, 1972.

Miner, Margaret and Hugh Rawson, eds. *American Heritage Dictionary of American Quotations.* New York: Penguin Reference, 1997.

Moen, Lynn and Judy Laik, eds. *Around the Circle Gently.* Berkeley, CA: Celestial Art, 1995.

Mosley, Leonard. *Disney's World: A Biography.* New York: Stein and Day, 1985.

——. *Lindbergh: A Biography.* Garden City, NY: Doubleday, 1976.

Mullane, Deirdre, ed. *Words to Make My Dream Children Live: A Book of African-American Quotations.* New York: Anchor Books, 1995.

Mumford, Lewis. *The Brown Decades: A Study of the Arts in America, 1865-1895.* New York: Harcourt, Brace and Company, 1931.

Nixon, Richard. *The Memoirs of Richard Nixon.* New York: Grosset & Dunlap, 1978.

Oates, Stephen B. *Let the Trumpet Sound: The Life of Martin Luther King Jr.* New York: Harper & Row, 1987.

Pasquariello, Ronald D., ed. *Almanac of Quotable Quotes from 1990.* Englewood Cliffs, NJ: Prentice Hall, 1991.

Pepper, Frank S., ed. *The Wit and Wisdom of the 20th Century: A Dictionary of Quotations.* New York: P. Bedrick Books, 1987.

Peter, Laurence J. *Ideas For Our Time.* New York: William Morrow and Company, Inc., 1977.

Plimpton, George, ed. *Writers at Work: Second Series.* New York: Penguin Books, 1963.

——. "Points to Ponder," *Reader's Digest* (August 1970): 126.

Powell, A. C. *Adam by Adam: The Autobiography of Adam Clayton Powell, Jr.* New York: Dial Press, 1971.

Powell, Colin L. *My American Journey: A Dictionary of Quotations.* New York: Garland Publishing, 1995.

Powell, David. *The Wisdom of the Novel.* New York: Garland Publishing, 1985.

Powell, Joanna, ed. *Things I Should Have Said to My Father: Poignant, Funny and Unforgettable Remembrances from Memorable Sons.* New York: Avon Books, 1994.

Princeton Language Institute, ed. *21st Century Dictionary of Quotations.* New York: Dell Publishing, 1993.

Quindlen, Anna. *Living Out Loud.* New York: Random House, 1988.

Reader's Digest, ed. *Reader's Digest Quotable Quotes: Wit and Wisdom for All Occasions From America's Most Popular Magazine.* Pleasantville, NY: Reader's Digest Press, 1997.

——. *Reader's Digest Treasury of Modern Quotes.* Pleasantville, NY: Reader's Digest Press, 1975.

Reagan, Ronald. *The Wisdom & Humor of the Great Communicator.* San Francisco: Collins Publishers, 1995.

Riley, Dorothy Winbush, ed. *My Soul Looks Back, 'Less I Forget—A Collection of Quotations by People of Color.* New York: HarperCollins, 1993.

Robinson, Sharon. *Stealing Home.* New York: HarperCollins, 1996.

Rockefeller, John D. III. Speech at Family of Man awards dinner, October 1968, as quoted in "We Need Our Young Activists," *Reader's Digest* (August 1970): 53-57.

"Rock On." *People* 48, no. 2 (July 14, 1997): 133.

Rogers, Fred and Barry Head. *Mister Rogers Talks with Parents.* New York: Berkley Books, 1983.

Safire, William and Leonard Safir, eds. *Words of Wisdom: More Good Advice.* New York: Simon & Schuster, 1989.

Sandburg, Carl. *The Letters of Carl Sandburg.* New York: Harcourt, Brace & World, 1968.

Schickel, Richard. *Clint Eastwood: A Biography.* New York: Knopf, 1996.

Shapiro, Nat, ed. *Whatever It Is, I'm Against It.* New York: Simon & Schuster, 1984.

Sherline, Reid, ed. *Love Anyhow: Famous Fathers Write to Their Children.* New York: Timken Publishers, 1994.

Simpson, James Beasley, ed. *Simpson's Contemporary Quotations: The Most Notable Quotes from 1950 to the Present.* New York: HarperCollins, 1997.

Spock, Benjamin and Steven J. Y. Parker. *Dr. Spock's Baby and Child Care.* New York: Pocket Books, 1998.

Stevenson, Burton Egbert, ed. *The Homebook of Quotations: Classical and Modern.* New York: Dodd, Mead and Company, 1967.

Stewart, Meiji, ed. *Parenting: Part Joy, Part Guerrilla Warfare.* Del Mar, CA: Keep Coming Back Company, 1997.

Szasz, Thomas. *The Second Sin.* Garden City, NY: Anchor Press, 1973.

Toffler, Alvin. *Future Shock.* New York: Random House, 1970.

Toomer, Jean. *Essentials.* Edited by Rudolph P. Byrd. Athens, GA: University of Georgia Press, 1991.

Tripp, Rhoda Thomas, ed. *International Thesaurus of Quotations.* New York: Thomas Y. Crowell, 1970.

Truman, Margaret. *Letters From Father.* New York: Arbor House, 1981.

Twain, Mark. *Mark Twain's Book for Bad Boys & Girls.* Chicago: Contemporary Books, 1995.

Updike, John. *Assorted Prose.* New York: Knopf, 1965.

Washington Post, January 25, 1993, Sec. A, p. 11, col.1.

Watson, Thomas J. Jr. *Father, Son & Co.: My Life at IBM and Beyond.* New York: Bantam, 1990.

Webster's Dictionary of Quotations. New York: Smithmark, 1995.

Weiser, Marjorie P. K., ed. *Pegs to Hang Ideas On: A Book of Quotations.* New York: Evans, 1973.

Weiss, Irving and Anne D. Weiss, eds. *Reflections on Childhood: A Quotations Dictionary.* Santa Barbara, CA: ABC-CLIO, 1991.

West, Bob, ed. *Loving Children: Words of Love About Kids From Those Who Cherish Them.* San Francisco: Halo Books, 1993.

Williams, William Carlos. *The Selected Letters of William Carlos Williams.* Edited with an introduction by John C. Thirwall. New York: McDowell, Osolensky, 1957.

Willis, Andre C., ed. *Faith of Our Fathers: African-American Men Reflect on Fatherhood.* New York: Dutton, 1996.

Winokur, John, ed. *Fathers.* New York: Penguin Books, 1994.

——. *Friendly Advice.* New York: Penguin Books, 1990.

Woods, Earl. *Training a Tiger: A Father's Guide to Raising a Winner in Both Golf and Life.* New York: HarperCollins, 1997.

Wright, John Lloyd. *My Father Who Is on Earth.* New York: Putnam, 1962.

Young, Andrew. *A Way Out of No Way.* Nashville: Thomas Nelson, 1994.

Zall, Paul M., ed. *The Wit & Wisdom of the Founding Fathers.* Hopewell, NJ: Ecco Press, 1996.